Stock Market Investing for Beginners:

The Best Book on Stock Investments To Help You Make Money In Less Than 1 Hour a Day

Table of contents

Part 5: Critical investment lessons...........................111

6

an illegal act irrespective of if it is done electronically or in print. This extends to creating a secondary or tertiary copy of the work or a recorded copy and is only allowed with the express written consent from the Publisher. All additional right reserved.

The information in the following pages is broadly considered to be a truthful and accurate account of facts and as such any inattention, use or misuse of the information in question by the reader will render any resulting actions solely under their purview. There are no scenarios in which the publisher or the original author of this work can be in any fashion deemed liable for any hardship or damages that may befall them after undertaking information described herein.

Additionally, the information in the following pages is intended only for informational purposes and should thus be thought of as universal. As befitting its nature, it is presented without assurance regarding its prolonged validity or interim quality. Trademarks that are mentioned are done without written consent and can in no way be considered an endorsement from the trademark holder.

Introduction

The stock market refers to all the parties involved in the buying and selling of shares of publicly listed companies, bonds, and other securities. It is a vital component of the free economy. It consists of two main segments: the primary market and the secondary market.

The primary market is made up of mainly early-stage companies seeking resources through the sale of shares in what is known as IPOs. Thanks to the stock market, companies may acquire funds by selling stock to public investors in exchange for part ownership.

The market is on an upward trajectory and more investors are turning to stocks. This implies that the stock market is an incredibly profitable niche. Actually, the third richest man in the world, Warren Buffett, made his fortune through investing in the stock market. But the main difference between Warren Buffett and other investors is down to discipline and rationality.

Making money from the stock market is not as hard as people make it out to be. Like any other field, it can be mastered, and the only real way of mastering stock markets is through study and practice. Many investors make a killing out of stock markets. In the same vein, many investors commit their resources to bad investments and lose it all.

The stock market can be a very unforgiving pursuit, and in order to realize a profit, you must be armed with not just pedestrian investment tips, but solid information.

This book details all the basics of stock market investing and shows you how to get started.

Part 1: The Essentials of Stock Market Investment

Chapter 1:
Investment vs. Speculation

In the 1934 classic book, *Security Analysis*, Ben Graham says, *"An investment operation is one which, upon thorough analysis, promises safety of principal and a satisfactory return. Operations not meeting these requirements are speculative."*

In simple terms, an investor is a person who determines to make their money work for them. For instance, they may use their savings to purchase, a percentage of a company, and thus be entitled to a share of the company's profits for as long as they retain ownership.

The average employee must work for their money. They exchange their time and skills for money. Unlike employees, money doesn't tire, doesn't catch an illness, doesn't develop moods, or doesn't get bored, and so it has the distinction of having a 24-hour utility. An investor should know how to put money into use in such a manner that it will earn him great returns.

An often prevalent misconception is that investing is a preserve of the high and mighty. It's true that millionaires and billionaires are into it, but it doesn't mean that it is *their* preserve. Any person who has a reasonable amount of cash is a very good candidate for being an investor. But like anywhere else, investing has its rules, and it's only the people who stick to the rules who end up beating the system.

When you fail to act within the rules of investing, you might unbeknownst to you become a mere speculator. A speculator is interested in only short gains. Speculators are proverbially carried by the wind and they tend to rush in markets where they can make a killing in as short amount of time as possible. For this reason, speculators are vulnerable, and they constantly fall prey to market frauds. For instance, in mid-2017, the price of a cryptocurrency known as Bitcoin had experienced an artificially engineered surge, and some speculators went so far as to even sell their property and buy bitcoin in hopes of making a massive overnight return. They hadn't known that they were getting sucked into a bubble, but soon enough, the bubble blew up, and the lofty dreams of all of those speculators came crashing down. An ocean of tears was shed and lives were ruined.

The father of value investing, Ben Graham, said, "There are many ways in which speculation may be unintelligent. Of these, the foremost are: (1) speculating when you think you're investing; (2) speculating seriously instead of as a pastime when you lack proper knowledge and skill for it; and (3) risking more money in speculation than you can afford to lose."

The main obligation of an investor is to analyze in detail the long-term potential of a particular business endeavor and then decide whether to commit their resources into that endeavor. The goal of every investor is to earn a good return on their investment.

Some of the popular long-term investments include:

- **Stocks**
- **Bonds**
- **Mutual funds**
- **ETFs**
- **Alternative investments**

Chapter 2:

Understanding the Stock Market

The stock market plays a critical role in driving the economy. It is characterized by the trading of equities of publicly listed companies and other securities. A popular investment style sees investors pumping their funds into a public company in exchange for part or full ownership of the company. Thus the investors are entitled to a share of the company profits. In this vein, a successful investor is one that receives more in the way of dividends than the capital they initially gave out. The stock market is divided into two categories, namely, primary and secondary capital markets.

Primary market: this is where shares or equities are traded via an initial public offering (IPO) i.e. investors trade directly with the company.

Secondary market: investors trade among themselves while the company associated with the traded security is excluded from the trading.

The two factors that determine the price of a public company's IPO stock are the value of the company and the volume of shares.

The company may stash away its IPO windfall, but once its stock trading grows enough to generate revenue, the company doesn't profit. The stock trading of most companies is normally carried out on exchanges. Exchanges play the role of facilitating trade between buyers and sellers. Thanks to new technology, exchanges now list stocks in electronic format.

Stock market exchanges are found in almost any capital city in the world. In the U.S., there are two major stock exchanges: the **New York Stock Exchange** and the **Nasdaq.**

The Securities and Exchange Commission, an independent federal agency, oversees the exchanges in the U.S. to enforce fair play and protect the rights of the investors.

Investors who are constrained by cash, usually thrive in exchanges as opposed to IPOs. IPOs prefer working with large investment vehicles (for instance Berkshire Hathaway) as opposed to small two-thousand-in-the-bank investors. But the exchanges welcome anyone to purchase securities. Investors may get in on the action themselves or they might hire brokers.

The stock price is driven by supply and demand forces. For instance, if there's a lot of buzz around a company, and there are lots people wanting to buy shares of that company, the share price will go up, and the same is true for profitable companies too.

Types of shares:

- **Ordinary shares**
- **B-Ordinary shares**
- **N-Ordinary shares**
- **Preference shares**
- **Exchange traded funds**

The two primary types of securities traded on the stock market are **listed securities** and **over-the-counter** (OTC). Listed securities must meet the requirements of the exchange and must also receive approval from the Securities and Exchange Commission.

On the other hand, over-the-counter securities are traded between peers, where the trades are usually facilitated by dealers. Over-the-counter securities don't appear on exchanges and they don't have to fulfill SEC requirements.

There's always an underlying element of risk in investments. You risk losing it all or not making as much profit as you had anticipated. Warren Buffett, the legendary investor, warned that risk came from not knowing enough.

Reading financial journals, attending investor workshops, and hiring professionals are some of the techniques you can use to minimize or eliminate risk from your decision.

Some products and securities are riskier than others. For instance, cash in the bank, government bonds, and ETFs are considered to have low risk, whereas corporate bonds, shares, and derivatives are considered high-risk. On the brighter side, a high-risk investment has the potential of being exceedingly profitable. The best protective measure against failure is to diversify. A diverse investment portfolio helps you absorb the loss and also speeds up wealth creation.

The main players in the stock market include:

- **Stockbrokers**
- **Stock analysts**
- **Investment bankers**
- **Portfolio managers**

Chapter 3:

Make More Money and Take Fewer Risks with Mutual Funds

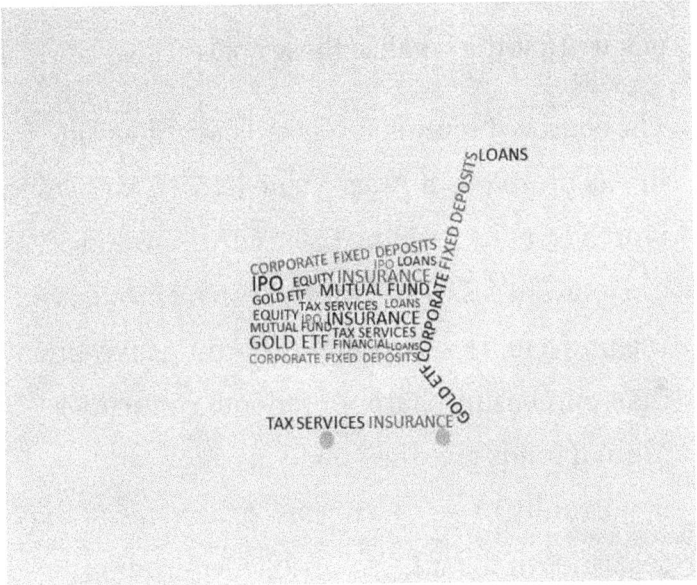

Mutual funds appeal to investors who have the mind of unity as opposed to striking it alone. Mutual funds are high-flying projects in which resources are pooled together for the purpose of a scaled securities investment. The funds are contributed by investors in exchange for a slice of ownership of the fund. The fund is directed by qualified personnel known as a fund manager. The investment decisions are made by the manager, with the board acting as the authorizing body. Generally, a mutual fund must have goals, and it is upon the fund manager to ensure that they realize these goals.

The shares of mutual funds are bought at the fund's present Net Asset Value (NAV). This value is arrived at by dividing the securities value of the total shares. Having a stake in a mutual fund is a much more secure and rewarding investment than purchasing shares of random companies. Mutual funds give the "small investor" an opportunity to own a portion of the value of the securities in the fund's portfolio, which improves their odds of making money, considering that fund managers are some of the few people who are incredibly skilled at making consistently high-returns investment choices. But this should not be misconstrued to mean that mutual funds hardly ever go into losses.

Basically, mutual funds pool money together sourced from many investors, which puts the company's financial muscle on steroids. The manager of the fund can select which securities to invest in. The value of the company depends on the tidings realized from the investments in securities. In that sense, a mutual fund is both an investment and a company.

Mutual funds investments in securities are typically wide-ranging. And so an investor who owns shares of a mutual fund enjoys the advantage of diversification. This is a far cry from what solo investors have. For instance, a person who has bought Apple stocks would suffer great losses if the company were to collapse. However, a person who has ownership of shares of a mutual fund is likely to emerge unscathed when their company makes a loss from a specific investment because their company holds a wide range of investments.

Types of mutual funds:

- Fixed income
- Index funds
- Balanced funds
- Money market funds
- Sector funds
- Equity funds
- Alternative funds
- Smart-beta funds
- Target-date funds
- Funds-of-funds

A fund normally distributes its income to shareholders over the year. The shareholders have the option of receiving cold cash or reinvesting. Here are the three ways in which a mutual fund investor earns:

- They may receive shareholder dividends and the interest on bonds.
- If the fund sells its securities at a higher price, part of the income generated is distributed amongst shareholders.

- If the value of the fund goes up as a result of investment in securities, the fund's share prices go up too, in that way an investor would sell their shares at a higher price.

Reasons why investing in mutual funds are far better than purchasing stock:

Professional management. The average investor probably has no time, skills, and information to make an educated investment decision. But a mutual fund is controlled by an able manager who should make the best decisions on your behalf.

Diversification. Mutual funds invest in a wide range of securities, thus spreading the risk.

Economies of scale. A mutual fund buys and sells in large volumes and so they are entitled to reduced fees. Also, a mutual fund has the capacity to invest in big proportions as opposed to what a single person could have managed.

Simple. In this age of technology, buying a mutual fund is a few clicks away.

Transparency. They are regulated.

Ease of access. Mutual funds can be purchased and sold with ease on exchanges.

Custom. An investor has the liberty to scout for a mutual fund that aligns with him even philosophically.

Chapter 4:

What are Index Funds and ETFs?

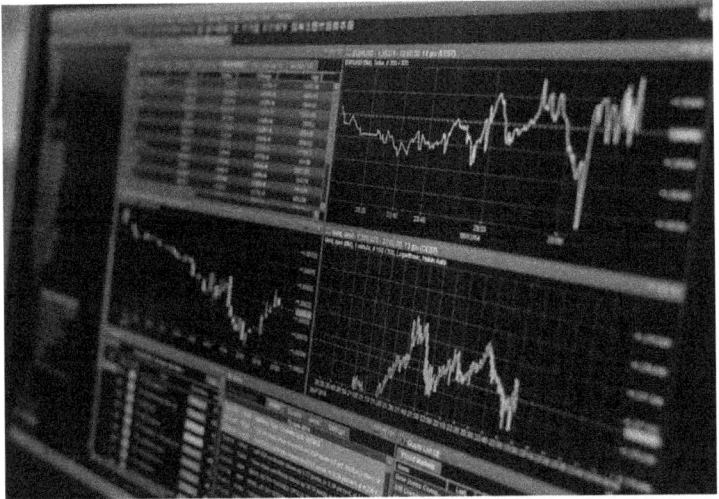

An *index* refers to the collective securities that represent the value of an economic sector. Investors track indices in order to determine how well or badly a market sector is doing.

An *index fund* is a collection of securities investments that involves tracking of market performance. Investors gain when the market goes up. Index funds are a viable investment path because they offer wide exposure in the market and considerably lower expenses, as opposed to, for instance, hedge funds.

As a form of passive fund management, index funds sometimes bring more gains than the highly bureaucratic mutual funds. The majority of index funds track the S&P 500.

Before purchasing an index fund, an investor should first understand the index, and also check the rate in which an index fund replicates the gains of its index. Although an index fund is considered a passive form of investing, it is upon the portfolio manager to say how the fund will track the index.

Some funds may seek gains from an index by investing in the constituent securities of that index, while other funds may seek gains by purchasing securities that appear similar to the securities within its index, and moreover, some funds may replicate an index by use of other financial instruments.

An *exchange-traded-fund* (ETF) is a collection of securities investments whose shares may be purchased or sold on an exchange at the set market price. An ETF is similar to a mutual fund in the sense that it collects resources from many investors and then invests in the best-performing markets. An ETF must have an investment goal and a sense of direction.

Most ETFs only ever invest in securities and must operate within the guidelines set by the Securities and Exchange Commission (SEC).

Types of ETFs:

- Broad market
- Sector and industry
- International
- Commodities
- Currency
- Dividend and income
- Fixed income/bonds
- Passive or active management
- Leveraged or hedged strategies

- Factor-based strategies
- Capitalization-weighted

ETFs are listed on exchanges and you may purchase or sell shares during trading hours. The price of ETF is determined by market forces, unlike mutual funds whose share prices are determined by the Net Asset Value (NAV) which is calculated at the close of the trading day.

Benefits of ETFs:

- You may buy ETFs through your broker at any time during trading hours.
- ETFs promotes portfolio diversification. ETFs confers securities to investors in various sectors, markets, and asset classes.
- The operating fees are significantly lower than mutual fund and hedge fund fees.
- ETFs are highly liquid partly due to their quick tradability on exchanges.
- ETFs has accurate price tracking.

Important things to evaluate before investing in an ETF:

- Objectives
- Risks
- Costs

An ETF generally has an objective that it proudly states. It is upon you to judge whether the strategies that the sponsor employs are worthy or not.

As a securities investment pool, ETFs carry an element of risk. The main risks are associated with uncontrollable factors, for instance, market failure, currency fluctuations or inflation. But also watch out that you don't fall prey to scams!

Some of the fees associated with ETFs include:

- Administrative
- Advisory
- Fund operating expenses
- Brokerage commissions

- Bids
- Premium/discount volatility

Chapter 5:
Secrets of Investing in IPOs

An *initial public offering* (IPO) is a popular method of raising investment capital and it involves a company selling its stock to the public for the first time. IPOs are commonly sought by early-stage companies in order to gain capital for expanding their operations. IPOs may also be sought by private companies that want to become publicly traded, thus the common phrase, "Going public."

IPOs offer the common public a chance to own the company. Prior to the issuance of an IPO, a company is considered private, since the people holding a stake in the company are likely a compact group consisting of founders and angel investors.

Some of the reasons a company goes public include:

- Access to greater funds.
- It promotes a more liquid and diverse share capital base.
- It strengthens brand image and credibility.
- Puts the company in a position to acquire other companies in the future.
- There's a higher valuation due to the release of documents and elimination of uncertainty.
- Provides liquidity for investors.
- Rewards its performing management through share options.

- Fosters the company's competitive edge.
- Debt reduction opportunity.

For an average investor, buying stock from a company may be a rarity, but still, some investors luck out. To understand why it is a rarity, you have to remember that a company's interest is raising about as much money as it possibly can. And so a company would rather get the big-buck institutions to buy stock rather than thousands of investors. Selling a million shares to an institution is way more efficient than finding thousands of investors to buy shares. Also, many investors lose out on a chance to invest in IPOs because the brokers that the company works with are more likely to "take the deal" to the investors in their circles.

In this way, your chances of getting in on the IPO action result in a big part on having a well-connected broker with whom you're in good standing. Brokers tend to have many clients and they may be biased against some of their clients. Beyond this, you could also try to approach the founders of a company and request for a consideration in IPO offers.

But simply because you have a chance to invest in IPOs doesn't automatically mean that you will earn a profit. Take some of these measures to get out of harm's way.

Be cautious. If your broker asks you to invest in a certain IPO, don't just run for it like a madman, but take your time to see that it is the right decision.

Vet the top management. If the executives are newsmakers in a negative light, time to boot. You can't commit your monies to someone who, for instance, rapes interns.

Go for the big fish. Big firms have an image to protect but the small fish couldn't care less.

Do your research. It can be hard finding information about a company that is going public. But that doesn't excuse the fact that you must dig hard enough and uncover relevant information touching upon the company's inner workings, financial health, and business practices. Research brings up stuff that either solidifies your interest or puts you off.

Read the prospectus. It is not the most interesting stuff to read, but you should go through it if only to understand the company's direction, risks, and opportunities.

Part 2: Maximize Returns from your Stock Selection

Chapter 6:
How to Make Money from Fundamental Analysis

Fundamental analysis is the study of the fiscal data of a company. The aim is to determine the financial health and performance of a company, as well as project, whether a company will be strong or weak in the future. Fundamental analysis is a critical financial exercise because it empowers the investor and helps them decide whether or not to invest. It is **fundamental** to success in securities investing.

Fundamental analysis could be employed in any kind of securities valuation, although most investors tend to confine it in stock valuation. Some of the key metrics taken into account include income, profit margins, interest rates and projected future growth.

A thorough evaluation of the financial statements of a company helps to draw an accurate conclusion.

An investor who is proficient at making fundamental analysis has an unfair advantage over the rest. Warren Buffett, also known as the Oracle of Omaha, made his incalculable fortune through buying off companies that he estimated would be successful in the future. But what made his predictions so accurate? It is an open secret that fundamental analysis would help him arrive at these decisions.

Interestingly, some investors use shallow and unscientific techniques to evaluate companies' performance, overlooking a time-tested method like fundamental analysis. The reasons for this might be that they lack the skill or time or even the concern, which is a mistake. The initial effort required at the start of making an investment is usually larger, but thereafter one is rewarded with a passive income.

It is important to have the tools for fundamental analysis in order to look beyond the results at face-value. The tools extrapolate on market value, earnings, and growth. Some of the most important factors to consider include:

Earnings per share. What percentage of profit is assigned to the shares?

Price-to-earnings ratio. What is the current share price to its earnings per share?

Projected earnings growth. By what percentage will the stock grow within an annual time-frame?

Price-to-sales ratio. What is the share price compared to the revenue of the corporation?

Price-to-book ratio. What is the book value of the stock compared to its market value?

Dividend payout ratio. What is the amount of dividends paid out to shareholders compared to the company's income?

Dividend yield. What are the yearly dividends compared to stock prices?

Return on equity. What is the company's return on equity? This figure is found by dividing a company's net income by stockholders' equity.

Always remember that these numbers play the role in shaping your judgment and must be used wholly, not disjointly, and are thus a yardstick for measuring the income-potential of a particular investment.

It is a better idea to wade through the waters of security's, investing guided by something more than just your gut feeling: fundamental analysis. Even if you perceive yourself as illiterate in matters of finance, you must not allow that attitude to hold you back from becoming your own stock market analyst.

While fundamental analysis focuses on securities valuation by studying financial statements of a company, technical analysis merely study market forces and their impact on securities value.

Chapter 7:

Quick Due Diligence, Medium Due Diligence,

and Full Due Diligence

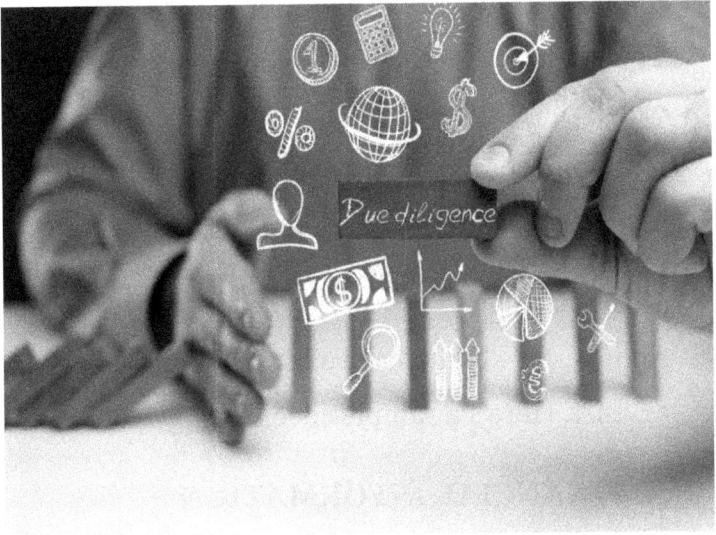

Due diligence is the process of vetting the authenticity of an investment. It is made in order to eliminate debt from the parties to a transaction. Due diligence is normally carried out when there's a deal on the table, but the parties to that deal have not sealed a contract yet.

In the world of securities investments, due diligence is carried out by fund managers, brokers, stock analysts, and investors. It is a highly recommended operation for investors. You get to assess the value of an investment and weigh the associated risks. Also, you get served with important company documents that may reveal insider information that would not have been otherwise available.

An investor should have a list of metrics to check against. Here's a sample checklist:

A) FINANCIAL INFORMATION

1. Annual and quarterly fiscal information

- Income statements, cash flows, and balance sheets
- Plans vs. results
- Financial reports of management

- Sales and profit breakdown by location, type of product, and channel
- Customer backlog
- Accounts receivable

2. Economic performance projections

- Quarterly economic performance projections: revenue and income statements.
- The major drivers of growth and prospects
- Business predictability
- Foreign operations risks e.g. national instability
- The pricing policies of industry and company
- The economic assumptions
- Capital expenditure projections and capital arrangements
- External finance

3. Capital structure

- Outstanding shares
- Shareholder list
- Debt instruments
- Liabilities off balance sheet

4. Other information

- Tax positions
- Operating loss
- Accounting policies
- Relevant financing history

B) PRODUCTS

1. Product description

- Major applications
- The growth rate projected
- Market share
- Nature and speed of technological change
- Product timing and enhancement
- Profitability and cost structure

C) INFORMATION ABOUT CUSTOMERS & SUPPLIERS

1. Top customers' name, location and address

2. Customers' relationship quality

3. Customers' individual revenue

4. Meaningful relationships that broke apart

5. Suppliers' list

6. Suppliers' relationship quality

D) COMPETITION

1. Landscape of competition in each segment

- Competition basis
- Market position

E) SALES, MARKETING AND DISTRIBUTION

1. Strategy

- Local and international distribution channels
- Company products and positioning
- Market opportunities
- Associated risks
- Marketing programs

2. Customers

- Relationship statuses and trends
- Future growth prospects and development
- Analysis

3. Main ways of generating new business

4. Model of productivity

- New workers
- Cycle of sales
- Compensation

5. Market plan implementation within given budget

F) RESEARCH AND DEVELOPMENT

1. Organization description

- Main activities
- Principals
- strategies

2. New products

- Timing and status
- Development costs
- Important technologies
- Associated risks

G) PERSONNEL AND MANAGEMENT

1. Management chart

2. Personnel numbers by location and role

3. Detailed profiles of senior management

4. Compensation plans

5. Management's incentive options

6. Important employee relations

7. Turnover of personnel

H) LEGAL MATTERS

1. Company lawsuits by aggrieved

2. Lawsuits filed by company

3. Environmental issues

4. Employee issues

5. Company liabilities

6. Intellectual property

- Copyrights
- Licenses
- Trademarks

7. Insurance cover

8. History of trouble with governing bodies e.g. Securities and Exchange Commission

Chapter 8:

Computation of Investment and Profitability Ratios

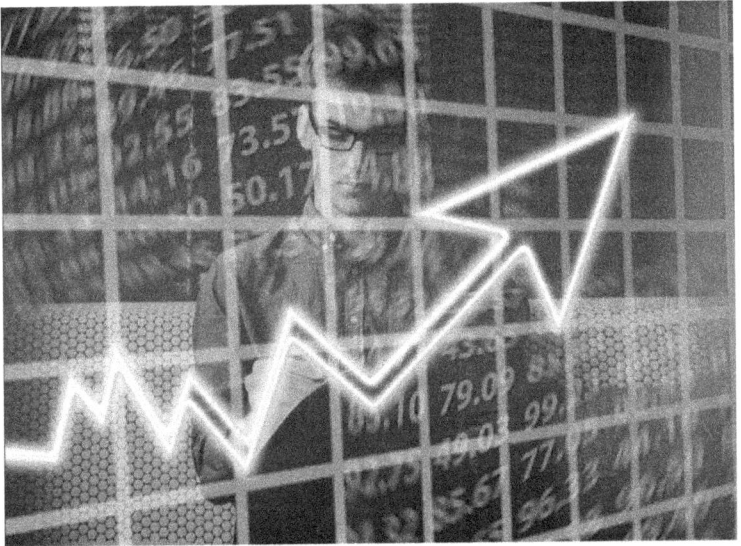

Whenever an investor commits their resources to an investment project, their intention is to generate a profit. The gains that an investor earns from an investment are known as return on investment (ROI).

Return on investment can be projected, too. A computation model is used to work out the projected gains and divides the gains by the original investment sum, thus finding the ratio.

ROI or return ratio is critical in helping an investor realize how their securities investments are stacked against the stock market. Investors like a simple metric for evaluating stock performance and profitability.

Profit is the income earned less the expenses, and it can be worked out in many different ways. A profit is the principal reason companies exist. A company that is profitable is assured of sticking around while a company that sustains a loss for a long time is likely to go out of business. ROI is what investors use to gauge their performance, and as an investor, it is always prudent to take action from reports where your investments are concerned, otherwise your investment career is at risk of going up in flames.

For instance, if Tim put $1500 of his savings into Milly's Computers, Inc. in 2017 and then sold his stock in 2018 for $2000 to get his return on investment, he would divide his profit ($500) by the initial investment sum ($1500) to get 33%.

Supposing that Tim had invested in other business projects, he might use the ROI from his investment in Milly's Computers, Inc. as a benchmark of the performance of his other investments.

Due to some limitations of the ROI method, some experts have proposed taking into account the social returns that an investment confers on an investor. This theory was developed in the early 2000s and it connects investments to social and environmental factors.

Margin ratios

- **Gross profit margin.** This metric allows investors to gauge a company's health by working out the money left over from income less cost of goods sold.
- **Operating margin.** This shows how much money is left over after deducting

both cost of goods and operating
expenses.

- **Net profit margin.** This is arrived at
after deducting operating expenses,
preferred stock dividends, interest, and
taxes, from a company's revenue.

- **Operating cash flow margin.** A
common method of working out
profitability ratios, this margin indicates
the money gained out of an investment
activity per every dollar in sales.

Returns ratios

- **Return on assets.** This shows the
company profits compared to company
assets.

- **Return on equity.** This method works
out how many dollars in profit a company
makes with each dollar of stockholders'
equity.

- **Cash return on assets.** A ratio that is
used in comparing the performance of a

business against other businesses in the industry. It is worked out by dividing the cash from investment operations of the company's total average assets.

The failure rate in companies is excessively high. And so, an investor ought to be very adept at researching companies and coming up with an accurate future valuation. An investor who's convinced that an investment has no capacity for profit is better off staying away from that investment.

Part 3: Strategies for Stock Market Investment

Chapter 9:
Winning Strategies of Investing in Stocks, Forex, Commodities, and Indices

Every successful investment management company has a hallowed business philosophy, but no matter how great their strategies are, there can never be a win-win situation unless you play your part well. There are many investment dynamics that are well within the control of an investor.

The average investor never appears concerned about playing his part well, especially if he has a broker or if he invests primarily in funds. He might express worry about the markets, the economy, manager popularity, or securities performances—which are greater things to worry about, actually—but when he fails to play his role, he lessens the momentum of everyone involved.

Folks, you have got to realize that there's no magic bullet, no one special trick that is going to eliminate all risk and guarantee you sky-high profits. The only way of reducing risk is by being competent. And you become competent through consuming relevant information and practicing.

The winning strategies are actually the default roles of an investor.

Goal. An investor should have a goal in mind. A great goal is both measurable and within reach. A goal should be well-defined and realistic and a path should be outlined for it. If an investor has no plan they will approach an investment piecemeal rather than push the entire portfolio for a common objective.

Balance. An investor should allocate assets using widely diversified funds. The asset allocation should fit into the portfolio's objective. The intelligent investor commits their resources on a number of business projects, thus spreading the risk. With a wide portfolio, the process of wealth creation becomes easier.

Minimize costs. The lower your costs, the bigger your share of returns. And research has shown that many low-cost investments have done better than higher-cost investments. An example of a lower-cost investment is purchasing index funds, which have a lower operating cost as compared to hedge funds and mutual funds.

Have discipline. This one cannot be overstated. When you invest, you might become vulnerable, especially when there is market turmoil. Investors react to shock-news by making impulsive investment decisions. You want to guard against that impulsivity. It'd be difficult to watch yourself without discipline. In as much as many people are killing it in the stock market, there are also others who are getting thrown down and stomped on, never rising again, and one would argue they lack discipline.

Evaluate your tax options. When you invest in funds, it is critical to assess your tax options. Always calculate the impact of taxes on your returns. The amount of tax levied will be affected by the type of your investment. Investing in funds attracts much more tax than purchasing shares.

Avoid mainstream media. Warren Buffett, the richest investor, spends his day reading books. He doesn't spend his day flipping from one channel to another, exposing his mind to the toxic world news. You might want to borrow a leaf from him. The mainstream media are negative on purpose. They aim to evoke people's emotions. You might consume too much negative media about the stock market and end up misleading yourself or even worse developing a negative outlook.

Fundamental analysis. Warren Buffett, again, the world's most successful investor is big on fundamental analysis, so why not you? Some people opt out of fundamental analysis on the complaint of not having a background in finance, failing to recognize that they could learn the concept or hire an expert. It has been said that fundamental analysis is fundamental to being able to make money in the stock market.

Chapter 10:
Principles of Value Investing

Ben Graham, the father of value investing once said, *"The intelligent investor is a realist who sells to optimists and buys from pessimists."*

Value investing is an investment strategy where an investor finds stocks that trade for less than their intrinsic value. Value investors vigorously look for stocks that they consider undervalued by the market. The idea is to swoop in early enough so that by the time a market segment awakens to the intrinsic value of the stock, the value investor will stand to make a large return on investment. Warren Buffett has made an incredibly large fortune out of being an excellent value investor.

Value investing varies from one person to another. Two investors can have wildly differing opinions on a similar investment. Some value investors tend to look at earnings and assets and place no value on projected future growth. Other value investors (Warren Buffett types) base their plans on future development of the company.

An illustration of the subjectivity of value investment:

On January 5, 2017, Glenn & Waters, Inc. released its Q1 2017 earnings report. Later, there was a steep decline in trading, which cost the company 19% of its value.

The company earned $500 million in the first quarter of 2017, which was a 50% rise from a year ago. The projected earnings of the company in the 2nd quarter of the year are $540 million.

The company is obviously healthy economic-wise and has great room for growth. However, since the company had a lot of development and research costs paid out in the 1st quarter of the year, earnings per share went down in comparison to the previous year.

Noticing this, some investors jump at the opportunity, selling off enough stock to cause a dip in share prices. All the while, a value investor understands that Glenn & Waters, Inc. is an undervalued company, with the potential of flourishing in the future.

Companies carry an intrinsic value. A value investor's main duty is to scout for companies that may be considered "weak" at present but in their assessment, these companies have a bright future. So, a value investor determines to work out the intrinsic value of the company.

Margin of safety. This is the difference between a stock's intrinsic value and its current market value. A value investor who purchases undervalued stock obviously gets entitled to a wide margin of safety in the event that stock prices go up, and yet they are unlikely to suffer a loss when the market doesn't perform as they'd hoped.

The efficient-market hypothesis is inaccurate. The efficient-market hypothesis states that all the relevant information about a company is reflected in its stock performance, and for that reason, there are no loopholes to beat the market. A value investor understands that a company's stock may sometimes be overvalued or undervalued. It is upon him to seek out the undervalued companies.

Never follow the herd. As Warren Buffett aptly said, "We simply attempt to be fearful when others are greedy and to be greedy only when others are fearful." The value investor bucks the trend.

Patience is important. A value investor never goes around devouring anything in his path. He understands that undervalued companies with a high intrinsic value don't come by easily. And so he waits until the appropriate company shows up in his radar.

Volatility is not necessarily risky. It may very well complement the value investment approach.

Chapter 11:

Margin of Safety and Competitive Edge in Growth Investment

Warren Buffett once said, "The three most important words in investing are 'margin of safety.'"

The margin of safety is the one thing that value investors are after, but what is it? The margin of safety is the difference between the market value of a stock and its intrinsic value. The margin of safety is found in undervalued investments that flourish at a later time.

Intrinsic value is the projected worth of an investment. It comprises an investment's estimated growth rate, future cash flow, and risk.

Working out the intrinsic value of an investment is not as easy as it may first seem. There are many variables that come into play. But the difficulty varies from one security to another. For instance, it is easier to calculate the intrinsic value of a bond than that of equity stock. The cash flow and duration of a bond is fixed. A stock has many variables that play a key role in its future performance. Generally, stocks call for a bigger margin of safety than bonds.

The main purpose of working out the intrinsic value is so as to profit from the undervalued assets. As it happens in these cases, the market value of an asset is down, and it encourages an investor to commit his resources to the investment. However, if the market value of an asset is beyond its intrinsic value, an investor would pass on that, as it is obviously overvalued.

The required margin of safety is the price beneath the intrinsic value that an investor is willing to purchase the asset at. The farther away the market price is from the intrinsic value, the bigger the margin of safety.

The key to a good investment is not to judge how much the asset is going to affect people but rather how much it will grow. An investor must identify the competitive edge of a company and then figure out how long the edge is going to last.

Payback time is the amount of time that you get to wait to realize profits from your investment. The payback time may vary from a few months to years. Seasoned investors are in it for the long haul, and they mostly invest their money so as to see gains for years as opposed to chasing a quick buck.

A value investor minimizes risk by requiring a discount on the purchase of stock. This is because an inaccurate intrinsic value and a small margin of safety together make a highly risky investment. Ultimately, the combination of low risk and big safety margin make an investment very worthwhile.

Two versions of the safety margin:

- Budget-based
- Unit-based

A margin of safety may offer a cushion against inaccuracies, but it certainly does not guarantee that an investment will be successful. The methods of arriving at this seemingly mythical "intrinsic value" vary among different investment personnel.

Chapter 12:
Basics of Income Investing

Income investing means committing your resources on investments with the aim of drawing a steady income over a certain length of time. Bonds and CDs are historically popular income investment choices, but in recent years the returns have been dwindling, sending investors to other investment avenues like purchasing equity.

The rise of income investing can be attributed in part to the social unrest of the 20th century. In the 20th century, there was so much racism, hostility, cruelty, oppression of women and so on. These hostility tendencies necessitated creating a way in which someone would be in control of their own finances, and thus income investing came about.

And since the labor markets tended to favor white men only, people would survive by owning stocks of various products. These companies would send dividends to stockholders throughout the year based on their equity stake and how well the company had performed.

Types of income investments:

Equity income funds

Equity income funds score, particularly high amongst cash-strapped investors. They are a great way to diversify your portfolio away from cash and bonds.

Global equity income funds

A global equity income fund offers diversified access to many companies and capital markets for income and growth of capital.

Multi-asset income funds

They can generate income from various sources, which can be held directly or in funds, investing across bonds, cash, and rental property.

Investment trusts

These are structured companies run by a manager and hold various assets such as shares and bonds across the securities markets.

Fixed income

Fixed income investments such as bonds are hugely favored especially by investors who like regular payments over a fixed period of time.

Property

This asset class achieves real income growth over the course of time. For instance, a landlord increases rents and the price of a property goes up.

Stock

Both common stocks and preferred stocks are great investment choices. When you purchase stock in a company, you take a slice of ownership of the company. This entitles you to a share of the company profits known as dividends. Before you buy stock, you may want to check the dividend payout ratios as well as the frequency of payment.

Bonds

You have a vast pool to select from— agency bonds, government bonds, municipal bonds, and savings bonds. Your personal taxable equivalent yield gets to establish whether you buy corporate or municipal bonds. Buying bonds with maturation dates of 5 to 8 years puts you at duration risk.

Real estate

You can be an owner of rental property or you can invest in property through real estate investment trusts.

What should investors look for in dividend stocks for an income investment?

- A reasonable dividend ratio. Generally, an investor who invests $30 to the company should have generated positive income.
- The track-record should be on an upward trajectory.
- A high return on equity with zero company debt. These can help you understand how the people take to businesses.

Why avoid the real estate investment?

- If the market falls, the loss is increased by leverage.
- There's potential for a lot of obstruction like lawsuits, maintenance, and insurance.
- Stocks have always performed better long-term than real estate.

Chapter 13:

Stock Market Tips and Tricks

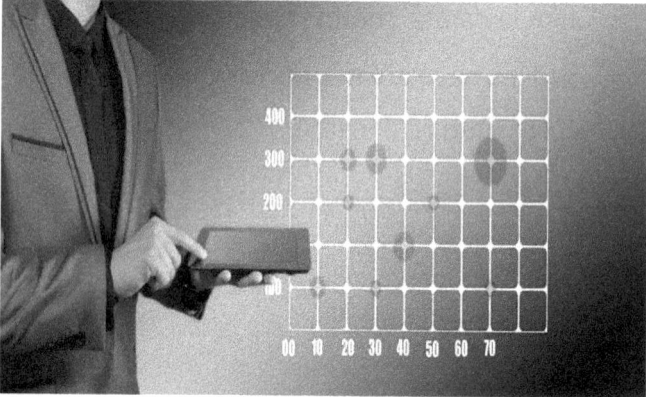

Right now, there are billions of dollars being generated throughout global stock markets. The stock markets are a very lucrative industry and at the same time very ruthless. It is a place where some men have made untold amounts of money while others have met their ruin.

Being successful in the stock market is not chalked to a fancy degree or the advice of your wealthy uncle. Stock markets reward knowledge and strategy.

Some people think that there's a quick buck to be made in trading stocks, and there's a name for them: speculators. Speculators often get burned when they try to play the system.

A great investor is not out to make a quick kill, but rather, he's there for the long haul. A great investor doesn't rush to eat anything that appears on his way. He's patient enough to wait for the fat calf which he will slaughter and eat to his fill.

No matter how skilled an investor might be, he too has a common enemy: risk. And one of the greatest favors he can do for himself is lowering the risk as much as possible.

Great investors know the value of discipline. Having discipline means not responding to news like a little puppy. It means not making impulsive decisions out of frustration. Having discipline amounts to operating within your guidelines and being true to yourself.

Stock market investment is not a reserve for the wealthy. Sure, there are many millionaires and billionaires throwing their monies into stock trading, but there's enough room for even "average investors."

Start early. Warren Buffett is the richest investor that ever lived. He made his first billion when he was well into his fifties. But the funny thing is that the Oracle of Omaha (Warren Buffett) had begun investing when he was a 10-year-old boy in Omaha. When you start early, you gain an unfair advantage over wide-eyed investors who come into stock trading a bit late.

Control the losses. Failing is a great part of moving forward. But don't fail so catastrophically that you cannot move any further ahead.

Check your emotions. Made a huge loss? Shut up. Made a fortune? Shut up. In truth, no one cares. Learn to not be overly emotional while reacting to market news.

Research is the secret. While most investors are happy taking wild rides and throwing their cash around and expect miracles, a great investor knows that investing is a hell of work, at least in the beginning, and heaviest part of it is doing research work. A great investor always researches on an investment first so that he may find as much information as need be before he finally reaches a decision. Knowing a hell lot about an investment certainly minimizes and even eliminates risk from the investment.

A great investor doesn't keep many balls in the air. They focus on a few high-value investments that are sure to give them enormous returns. When you juggle between a million investments, you end up losing your focus and becoming another victim of stock market ruthlessness.

Part 4: Stock Market Investment Approach

Chapter 14:
The Art of Short Selling

Short selling is the act of selling a security that one does not own. It is driven by the conviction that the security's value will go down over time and thus be able to be bought back to make a profit.

The equity-lending market plays the role of matching short sellers with stock owners willing to lend their shares at a cost. Apparently, there are many people who are interested in loaning out their shares and this industry is worth hundreds of billions!

Every investor wants to buy low and sell high. For instance, they may invest in stock, securities and wait for the price to go up. If they go up they may opt to sell their stock at a profit.

But there are times when markets experience strains that the stock price either dips or remains on a plateau. In these times, it is hard for an investor to make money taking advantage of the price difference.

And so, an investor may decide to borrow a security and sell it with the expectation of buying back shares later on at a reduced price to facilitate payment of the loan you'd taken.

Investors may short sell through brokerage firms. You place an order to sell the stock, and the broker inquires whether you are selling your own shares or short selling.

So, the brokerage allocates the investor's account shares borrowed from the market and then the sell order is executed. However, if the brokerage is unsuccessful in finding shares to loan your account, an investor will have to look in another market where loan-shares are available.

Once an investor sells the loaned shares, they wait for the security's price to lower, so they can buy the shares again at leverage. These newly bought shares are then returned to the original lender (through the broker) as loan payment, and you keep the difference as your earnings.

Stock exchanges have put in place regulations that discourage short selling shares that are moving down. And so, a short seller often finds himself swimming amongst the sharks.

Interestingly, the broker benefits of short selling when he charges transaction fees, but the actual owner of the shares might not even know that their shares had been loaned out.

Some of the risks associated with short selling include:

- **Short squeezes and "buy-ins."** A stock with high interest may experience price increment, which leads to unexpected losses on the part of the short seller.
- **Law.** Governing bodies might impose bans on short sellers in certain markets in order to prevent hysteria and protect the interests of traders. Such actions may cause a sudden rise in stock prices, thus the short seller sinks into losses.
- **Contrarian philosophy.** Short selling goes against the long-term market trend of prices moving up. Thus, a short seller is really gambling, and they have to execute

the short selling at the most appropriate time.

In the long run, most stocks tend to drift up, not down, and with that in mind, short selling attempts to go against the general market direction, which can result in huge losses.

Chapter 15:
Buying on Margin

Buying on margin simply refers to the act of borrowing money to purchase securities. An investor typically pays the margin and then borrows the remaining amount from a financial institution.

Buying on margin is typically made a down payment to the broker, while the investor's securities act as collateral for the borrowed money. An investor must first open a margin account with a broker before buying on margin.

In the U.S., the governing bodies require that an investor purchase assets with at least 50% in cash and then they might seek borrowed funds for the other 50%.

Before an investor can buy on margin, the broker must, first of all, determine the minimum amount of equity that must be kept in their margin account, and also they must determine the percentage of the purchase price of securities that the investor must pay in cash.

If an investor puts down $20000, the maintenance margin is 50% or $10000. If the equity of the investor goes even a dollar below $10000, the broker should ask him to restore the equity to the agreed maintenance margin ($10000).

When an investor's account dips below the maintenance margin, the investor may restore their account to an acceptable maintenance margin by putting in more cash or selling securities bought with a loan.

Are there any benefits associated with buying on margin?

Buying on margin may have its benefits to investors, but the practice is also steeped in risk. Considering that an investor borrows money to finance the purchase of their securities, unless the value of these securities increases, an investor could suffer loss especially if the securities' value goes down. Knowing this, an investor should utilize their buy, on margin option with securities whose value they are sure will go up.

Another huge benefit of buying on margin is that an investor has more investing options. With a cash account, an investor can only buy stocks or have basic options strategies. But in an account with margin maintenance, an investor has the chance to even exploit bear markets, through engaging in short selling. Also, an investor may dabble in all types of stock option strategies, which give you the right to purchase or trade a hundred shares of an underlying stock at a set price.

Of course, short selling and options trading are steeped in a lot of risks, but on the flip side, they carry a lot of potential for making a profit. An inexperienced investor should probably stick to buying stock and waiting for the price to shoot up. However, it is totally okay when an experienced investor explores the options strategy and short selling strategy with the intention of making a big profit.

There's no single investment strategy that can be termed as the best. Ultimately, it comes down to your level of tolerance for risk and your investment knowledge. If you're a newbie, then investing with margin would be akin to committing financial suicide.

Also, it'd be helpful to call on a broker, because a broker is incredibly knowledgeable.

Chapter 16:

Strategies for Making High Profits and Reducing Risk in Day Trading

Day trading is the act of buying and selling financial instruments—whether once or many times over—in the same day and seeking to make a profit from the fluctuating price. Day trading has the potential of making a lot of money and in the same breath has a high risk of losing money.

The first step is to of course familiarize yourself with the basic trading procedures. Traders should be in-the-know about the latest market news and other events affecting the stock market. You should always read up on matters touching upon your stocks of interest.

As a day trader, you cannot eliminate the element of risk. And so, you have got to set aside a portion of your money that you can afford to lose. Most successful traders are only willing to lose less than 1% of their account per trade. For instance, if you have a $20000 trading account, and are willing to risk 0.5% of your capital on each trade, your per trade maximum loss will be $100 (.005 * $20000).

Day trading is going to take your time—many hours, actually. A trader is required to study the markets and smell opportunities, which keep ebbing and flowing during trading hours.

The one beginner mistake for most traders is to start big instead of small. Your untrained mind can only catch up on one or two stocks during a trading session. It is easier to divide your attention between one or two stocks, any more than that would overwhelm your beginner's mind.

Stay away from penny stocks. Penny stocks are liquid and there's not that big a chance of making lots of money.

The worst time to make a move is when the price volatility kicks in. An experienced trader understands the price behavior and knows exactly when to make their move. But as a newbie, you might want to study the patterns first and then start making moves.

What are your entry and exit strategies? Will you use market orders or limit orders? A market order is implemented at the best price during execution, whereas a limit order guarantees the price but not the execution.

When you take up trading, ensure that you have no delusions. You don't have to win all the time in order to make a profit, but you should definitely ensure that your wins have big margins and your losses have smallest margins possible and the difference will put you ahead.

Learn to be grounded and rational. You might be tempted by greed or impulsive decisions, but such would only lead to a bad outcome.

What's your strategy? Oh, no, please don't just freewheel. You need to have a strategy for executing your trades and more importantly, you must adhere to that strategy. Whether you make a loss or profit, learn to move on quickly.

Three rules for the day trader:

- **Be flat at the end of the day.** You should liquidate all trading positions before you close the day.

- **End each day with a profit.** Your purpose of trading is to make a profit. Always aim high, but never worry when you close your day with a tiny profit; a profit is better than a loss.

- **Keep your losses small.** A big loss might harm days of hard work. Your priority is to always win. And if you must lose, it should be in a small margin.

Chapter 17:

Online Trading and Other Emerging Trends

Due to technology advancement, online trading has emerged to be popular among investors. There is software that tracks market performance and places trades and does pretty much everything.

The first thing you must do before trading stocks online is selecting an online broker. Your online broker will perform your trades and keep your money and stock in a secure online account.

There have been many mergers and acquisitions in the world of online trading, but still, there are many independent online firms to select from.

Different firms have diverse levels of assistance, types of accounts, platforms and other services. Before you start trading stocks online, here are some of the important things to keep in mind:

How much money do you have? Does your budget fit in with the requirements of your broker? Some firms will state the minimum deposit required and you must check to be sure that you comply.

How frequently will you trade? Are you going to purchase one type of stock and hold onto it dearly or are you going to be trading on the regular? If you are the kind that rarely trades, you might want to confirm that your broker doesn't charge your account for inactivity.

And if you are a regular trader, you might not want a broker that charges small fees per trade.

How experienced are you? Is this your first time doing this? Some brokers offer extensive guides to make you understand every aspect of online trading, but still, that doesn't make up for your lack of experience.

A tech website like Market Watch reviews the performance of brokerages based on rates of success, customer service quality, trading tools and other related factors.

Your broker will require your sensitive information, so make sure that the site is secure with SSL encryption and automatic logouts. Before you pick up a broker, try to read up on their online reviews to get what others are saying about them. A broker who receives tons of negative reviews is obviously problematic.

When you open an account with an online brokerage, you're required to answer a few questions about your financial and investment history.

The brokerage will determine which account is suitable for you. You will provide your social security number, telephone number, and address, in order to put your tax records in order.

You must then select your type of account: individual, joint, custodial or retirement.

Then you must choose between a cash account and a margin account.

Using a cash account, you have to have enough cash to buy stock, but with a margin account, you may have access to credit facilities based on the size of your stock equity.

Also, you must decide how the brokerage will keep your money from trade to trade. Many brokerages provide accounts with the capacity to earn interest, and you get to earn interest from your "idle" money.

Finally, you must fund your account in order to start trading. You can fund your account using wire transfer or any of the popular online payment methods.

When the brokerage activates your account, now you are set to trade.

Chapter 18:

Asset Valuation Principles & Portfolio Management

Asset valuation is the process of finding the worth of a company or any other valuable item. A big part of it involves measuring the assets that produce cash flow.

The advantages of getting an asset valuation include:

- **Having good knowledge of your assets.** An accurate asset valuation helps you understand what your assets are worth. This frees you to make bold investment choices.

- **Preparing for unforeseen investment opportunities.** Having an asset valuation prepares you for unforeseen investment opportunities where you'd ordinarily fail to give the accurate figure. In this way, asset valuation gives you more business.

- **Giving you more power.** Knowing the value of your assets helps you have a strong standing when negotiating a sale.

- **Evaluating the impact.** Having an asset valuation helps you weigh the impact that your assets have on your net worth.

- **Working out the returns.** Having an asset valuation helps an owner work out and compare the returns acquired from their assets.

Asset valuation is mainly carried out before the selling or buying of an asset or before buying insurance for an asset.

Some of the basis of asset valuation is transaction value, cash flows, and other valuation metrics.

Assets consist of securities and commodities, all of which have value. The measurements of working out asset value are both subjective and objective. For instance, it is difficult to quantify the worth of a company's brand by just looking at its financial statements because the brand is an intangible thing and thus valuation is subjective.

On the other hand, net income is an objective measure. If a company intends to acquire another company then its financial statements may be assessed and value known.

Analysts look at both book value and market value of assets. The book value is normally lower than the market value. The commonest way of asset valuation is connected to future cash flows.

Business valuation models:

- Asset-based model
- Earning value model
- Market value model

Asset-based model

It can be arrived at by subtracting total liabilities from the net value of assets or by working out the total amount acquired through liquidation of assets.

Earning value model

This model is based on the concept that the value of the company lies in its ability to generate future wealth. The most common model is through past earning capitalizing.

In this model, what an analyst basically does is to determine the future cash flow of a company by studying the past earnings of the company and multiplying its standardized cash flows by a capitalization factor.

The capitalization factor merely represents the rate of returns a buyer would expect from the investment.

Another formula of earning model is the discounted future earnings. In this model, rather than finding an average of past earnings, an average of projected future earnings is divided by the capitalization factor.

Market value model

In this model, a company is valued by comparing it to similar companies that lately sold. This method can be effective only if there are enough similar companies to act as a benchmark.

Part 5: Critical investment lessons

Chapter 19:

Can you survive on Wall Street?

Wall Street is not a random place on the map where you'd decide to just pack up your stuff and relocate. It is the financial market capital of the US, and by extension, the world.

Firms in Wall Street receive floods of resumes on a daily basis from people who hope to work in Wall Street, but guess what? 98% of all these job seekers get rejected as worthless.

In order to be considered, you will have to stand out. But before you get someone who's willing to even give you the chance to be heard, be prepared to send a ton of emails. With persistence and a bit of luck, you may land an interview and be on the way to working on Wall Street, where you'll be expected to prove yourself over and over again.

You might have heard of people that did courses like anthropology and literature in college, but went on to do great things on Wall Street. Well, such people are not in abundance. Most successful Wall Street figures have a degree in fields like math, finance, accounting, marketing, and economics.

You must target a number of firms and start reaching out to these firms either by phone, post, or email. The rejection rates are very high; don't let it bog you down, just shake it off and move on.

If you get a job in Wall Street, count yourself among the lucky few. But you may have gotten the job, but surviving there is an entirely different matter. If you turn out to be the lazy type, a cheat, a druggie, or exhibit some other vile behaviors, you will be given the boot.

Here are some tips that should help you succeed on Wall Street:

- **Resiliency.** Both physically and mentally. The investment world is a stress-laden industry. There's a small margin of people who survive on Wall Street as the majority are driven out of the place by market forces.
- **Adaptability.** Things move at a rapid pace; there's no stopping. You'll hardly be

doing the same thing that you were doing a year or two ago. The people change constantly, the markets shift, new opportunities come up, and in order to adjust to this kind of life, you have got to be adaptable, but with adaptability comes the need of being competent, and so you must ensure that you keep expanding your knowledge in order to qualify for the upgrades that might come your way from time to time.

- **Network**. Wall Street may admittedly be an awful place to make friends because money outs the beast inside every one of us. But at the same time, you must keep the effort to be in "speaking terms" with most people. If you put some effort into networking, you will have access to more deals and you will find yourself with so much work to do. Wall Street can be a cruel place and a lot of people quit and move elsewhere after a taste of what it's like.

- **Ruthless**. It may not be an admirable trait in a person, but in Wall Street, everyone is fighting their own war, and so you must keep your interests as the main priority. Never agree to be short-changed. Also, be economic with your kindness. As the star of Wall Street, Gordon Gekko said, "If you want a friend, get a dog."

Chapter 20: Top 20 Best-Performing Companies

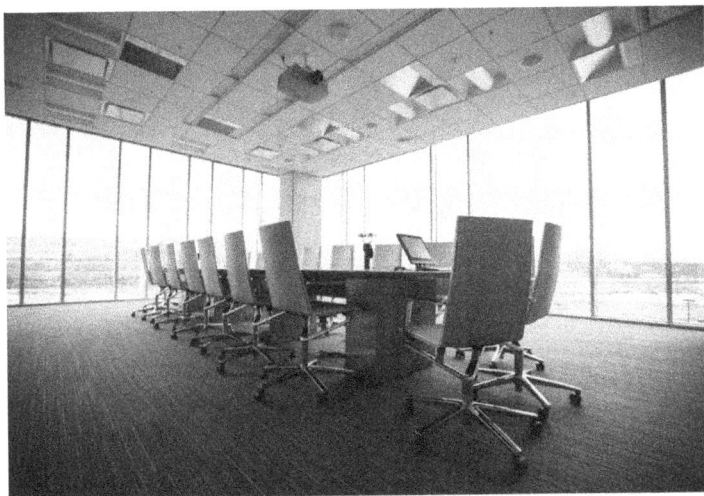

The purpose of going public for every company is to acquire more funds for their operations and expansion. But the aim of an investor is to make a profit. Investors buy stock with the expectation that the share price will go up and thus they will be at a point of selling their shares for a profit. There are many companies who have gone public and went ahead to lose investors' money, while there are other companies who have done exceedingly well. Here is a look at the 20 best-performing companies:

1. **ExxonMobil**

   This is an energy behemoth company. Studies show that the company has generated in excess of one trillion dollars since 1926. Shareholders of ExxonMobil are a happy lot since the company pays dividends handsomely.

2. **Apple**

   The company is synonymous with its moods and unpredictable co-founder, the late Steve Jobs. Apple is still the leader in tech markets under Tim Cook, and besides that, the company has the second best performing stock, with a market capitalization of close to one trillion dollars!

3. **Microsoft**

   Bill Gates dropped out of university to found this company together with his friend Paul Allen. Their first product went on sale in 1985. The following year, the company went public and, as they say, the rest was history. Microsoft stocks have pulled a staggering $629 billion.

4. **General Electric**

   The industrial conglomerate may not be performing exceptionally well at present, considering that even Warren Buffett sold his shares in 2017, but it has a storied history on the stock market. GE was one of the few companies to feature in the original Dow Jones industrial average. Its stock has garnered an estimated $608.1 billion.

5. **International Business Machine**

   IBM creates computer software and hardware. It is one of the longstanding tech companies and its products are a force to reckon with. It has not only survived in an environment of competition from Google, Microsoft, Amazon, and Oracle but also rounds up the top five best-performing stocks.

6. Altria

This American company is one of the biggest distributors of cigarettes, tobacco and other related products. Its stocks are some of the best-performing ones and the lifetime wealth creation stands at $470.2 billion.

7. Johnson & Johnson

Johnson & Johnson is a global company with products in health and pharmaceutical industries. Some of the most popular products of the company include Listerine, Tylenol, Johnson's baby oil, and Johnson's baby shampoo.

8. General Motors

General Motors may have suffered a bankruptcy in 2009 but that doesn't wave off the lifetime performance of its stock. GM went on to stage a comeback under a tough and able CEO, but the stock has not performed as bright as the days of yore.

9. Chevron

An energy conglomerate, the shareholders of Chevron are a happy folk considering that they have enjoyed 30 straight years of dividend increment.

10. **Walmart**

One of the world's biggest retailers, founded by a frugal man named Sam Walton. Walmart has the tenth best-performing stocks of all time.

11. **Alphabet**

This is the parent company of Google, and the performance of its stock is showstopping because Alphabet has been around only for so long.

12. **Berkshire Hathaway**

One of the true legends of the investment world, Warren Buffett bought a textile company in the 50s and used this company (Berkshire Hathaway) as his investment vehicle, acquiring countless businesses.

13. Procter and Gamble

The company has paid out dividends since the late 19ᵗʰ century and its lifetime wealth creation in the stock market stands at $355 billion.

14. Amazon

Amazon may have started as a simple website in the book niche, but Jeff Bezos has not only overseen its growth into one of the best-performing companies but also he's become the world's richest man in the process.

15. Coca-Cola

Coca-cola is almost like the Catholic Church; it has established a presence throughout the world. Its stocks are the 15ᵗʰ best performing of all time.

16. DuPont

It was founded in 1802 as a gunpowder mill by a French-American chemist. This chemical conglomerate has shown consistent performance in the stocks through time and has generated a wealth of about $308 billion.

17. AT & T Corp.

This is an American communication company that provides voice, video, and data services.

18. Merck

This pharmaceutical company was established in 1891 and had displayed consistent performance except in recent years the performance has relatively gone down.

19. Wells Fargo & Co.

Founded in 1852, Wells Fargo has been in the banking industry for quite a long time. The largest shareholder of Wells Fargo is Berkshire Hathaway, with a 10% stake.

20. Intel

A technology company renowned for making high-quality computer chips, Intel rounds up the top twenty best-performing companies in the stock market.

Chapter 21:

The Power of Diversification

Diversification is the investor's main defense against risk. An investor commits their resources to a wide range of investment categories. Diversification's main role may be to spread risk, but just as important is the ability to generate revenue.

Most investment professionals have said that diversification may not protect you 100% from loss, but it is a sure method of wealth creation and a dependable formula of attaining future financial goals while keeping risk at the minimum.

These are the two types of risks that investors face:

Undiversifiable. It is also referred to as "systematic risk," and it touches every company. The common risks in this category include high inflation rate, high exchange rate, political chaos, war, and high interest rates. This type of risk is beyond your control and there's no escape.

Diversifiable; also known as "unsystematic risk," it is category specific. This risk only touches certain companies, industries, markets, economies, and countries. This kind of risk can be effectively watered down through diversification. The unsystematic risk may be triggered by market forces or by poor investment decisions. Business risk and financial risk make up the most of unsystematic risk.

Case in point:

Let's say you have a portfolio investment of only Wells Fargo. When a major scandal rocks the company or when there is major market turmoil in the banking sector, their share price will tumble down. Your investment portfolio will lose significant value.

However, had you diversified your portfolio so that you had invested in securities in other economic sectors like airlines and railways and water companies, your investment portfolio would have absorbed the loss originating from the Wells Fargo deal.

Also, it is important that you diversify in different asset classes. For instance, bonds and stocks never give a similar reaction to unfavorable market conditions.

Diversification helps the market go up, thus improving index funds. When businesses have more resources, they may devote these resources to service delivery improvement and research and development of products. The world of investing embodies the idea of "one hand washing the other," and so businesses cannot make huge profits unless they have huge resources to optimize their products.

Diversification helps assess your performance. An investor who considers himself great needs to have proof of that. What better than to have a diverse portfolio? Having a diverse portfolio will help you make a judgment on your investment decisions. If a certain investment consistently shows great results while other investment consistently brings up poor results, you might want to sell off the poor investment and commit more resources to the investment that is doing well. This environment gives you a better idea of what works and you can gauge your ability to select performing investments.

Regulatory and legislative risks. There are some risks which exist outside of the markets, for instance, regulations and legislation. Some jurisdictions might come up with oppressive legislation or the governing bodies might develop new rules. If the rules have any adverse effects your portfolio would be a sort of cushion against the negative impact.

Investment diversification is the secret to fast-tracking wealth creation. Warren Buffett may not have become the greatest all-time investor if he'd chosen to focus on developing the textile company he'd acquired in the 50s.

Chapter 22:
Role of Technology in Trading & Profit Growth

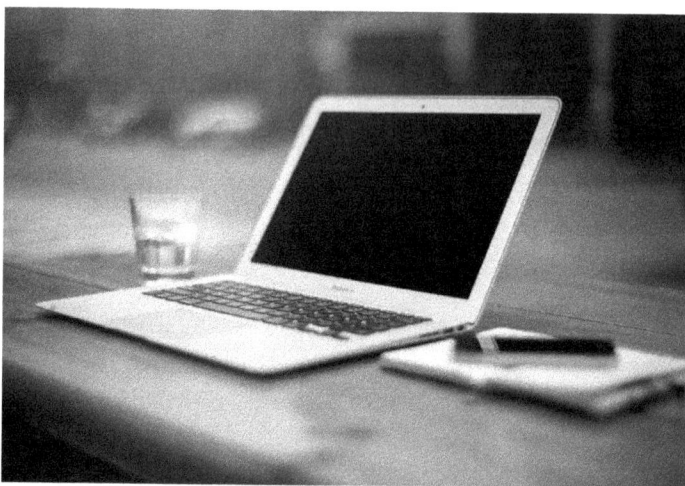

Technology has disrupted many sectors and the investment world is no exception. Even staunch anti-technology investors like Warren Buffett seem to have softened their stance on technology with his recent buying of Apple shares. It sends a message, technology is the future, and you either adapt or get thrown out.

Technology has helped companies evolve from targeting local markets into focusing on even an international consumer base. In many sectors, technology has improved on product creation and service delivery.

In the financial markets, the biggest role that technology plays is in data processing, storage, and other related services. The result of utilizing technology in financial markets has been high profits, smooth operations, and high client retention. Technology, it seems, is an aid to finance professionals, and not a threat as the uneducated person might want you to think.

Asset management has been a hands-on activity where fund managers select investments that they figure will generate the most profit for their clients. The dynamics of picking up the securities with the greatest potential are exhaustive. So, actively managing funds is a very resource-intensive undertaking, but what about passive fund's?

Passive funds differ from actively managed funds in the sense that the manager isn't very hands-on. An example of passive funds investment is index funds and exchange-traded-funds (ETFs).

The interesting thing is that investors are slowly ditching actively-managed funds and moving to passive funds. One of the obvious reasons is that passive funds attract significant administrative fees, but also, passive funds have a big room for technology optimization.

According to a research by PWC, passive investments will make up 35% of the asset management sector by 2020, chiefly because investors will seek low-fee investments and a large market exposure. And this development will affect the traditional asset managers who ask for high fees even though the investments of their clients are not always profitable.

Obviously, passive investments appeal to investors because of the added advantage of technological optimization.

There are existing technologies that manage investment funds automatically, placing trades and seeking maximum exposure all on autopilot. Normally, these technologies are software that you have to pay annual fees to obtain a license. Is the software accurate? It seems so, because there many online traders nowadays making a hell lot of money from automated trading.

The reason why traditional asset managers charge their clients a lot of money is simply because there's a lot of background work that goes toward making an investment profitable. Asset managers charge high fees because they pay researchers and analysts before reaching their decision and also they require adequate compensation for purposes of underscoring trust. However, automated program take the roles of researching, analyzing, detecting bad deals, placing trades, almost everything that an asset manager does, except that the robot advisor charges very low fees (annual software license fees).

As more advances are being made in the artificial intelligence sector, it is expected that powerful trading robots will be created, which can even outdo professional investors.

In such a scenario, the difference between making a loss and profit would not be chalked to humans, but the type of robot employed. But one thing is sure: robots will complement finance professionals rather than eliminate them.

Chapter 23:

The Role of a Stockbroker

A stock broker merely acts on the wishes of the investor. A stockbroker will connect a buyer to a seller and thus create liquidity. The work of a stockbroker is tough and it involves advising their clients on investment moves that will guarantee them high returns. A stock broker's activity for the day include researching, meeting clients, and being present on the floor for the trade executions. A broker's salary is in the form of commissions, and so his income might be quite unsteady.

A stock broker needs to have the right background in university and should have a degree related to these fields: business, economics, finance, and math. Also, they should have an extensive knowledge of the free markets and especially securities investments, as this is where most of their clients want to invest.

A stockbroker takes care of the needs of the investor. The following are the benchmarks for identifying a good stock broker:

- Experienced in public funds investing
- Skilled in competitive pricing
- Independent thinker
- Knowledge of the market
- Ability to make tactical and well-considered ideas
- Ability and willingness to inform you on important trends
- Owns important analytical tools

- Skilled at analyzing credit
- Skilled at economic research
- Skilled at income research
- Good execution of trades

The life of a stockbroker is hectic, and for good reason, they carry the hopes of many investors. Stockbrokers have great influence on the decisions of investors. Here are some of the roles of stockbrokers:

Contacting prospective clients. A stockbroker needs to have a client list, it doesn't matter whether they work individually or whether they work for a trading firm. So, they must put the effort in adding new clients to their list, following up on deals with current clients, and maintaining relationships with other industry professionals. Ideally, a successful stockbroker has an extensive network.

Trade executions. It is the duty of the stockbroker to buy or sell on behalf of their client. Nowadays, the stockbroker may buy or sell with just a push of the button on their computer, but in the days of yore, it was through phone calls or person to person.

Fair dealing. A stockbroker has a lot of information in his head. He could decide to use this information for illegal practices by luring naïve and unsuspecting investors. However, the regulatory authorities require that a stockbroker handles their client with transparency and in as fair a manner as possible. Stock brokers should not hold back critical information, especially when it's the kind that could influence the investor's decision.

Loyalty. A stockbroker earns through commissions. Sometimes, greed may come into the scene, leading to a clash between the interests of the stockbroker and those of their client. However, a stockbroker should at all time focus on the interests of their client first.

Supervision. A stockbroker has the duty of supervising their client's resources. This involves tracking developing trends and warning their client in case of an impending calamity. Stockbrokers have a great deal of information on their hands, and one thing hasn't said or one thing said makes a world of difference.

Chapter 24:
The Legends of the Stock Market

A great investor is a good master of money. The father of value investing, Ben Graham, is credited as inspiring modern investors and giving them the wisdom of investing intelligently. A successful investor is appreciated in the financial world, where success is mostly a result of hard work and a lucky break. These are the most successful investors of all time.

1. **Warren Buffett**

   The Oracle of Omaha is the faithful disciple of Ben Graham and he proudly says so. He's managed to accumulate a net worth of $81 billion through his investment vehicle, Berkshire Hathaway. Warren Buffett started investing at the age of 11 but it wasn't until his fifties that he made his first billion.

2. **George Soros**

   Born in Hungary, George Soros migrated to England and then to America where he made his fortune. George had started out working on the railway and in a hotel before he made the shift to the financial markets. His first job in finance was in a company named Singer & Friedlander in London.

3. **Prince Alwaleed Bin Talal Alsaud**

   A Saudi royal, Prince Alwaleed owns equities in multinational companies through his investment companies. In

2008, the prince was listed as one of the most influential people by Time's Magazine.

4. Carl Icahn

Carl Icahn began his financial career in Wall Street as a stockbroker. He'd later form his own securities firm and start buying stocks of companies. Some of the companies where he holds majority stocks include: RJR, Texaco, Nabisco, Gulf & Western, American Can, USX, Revlon, Marvel Comics and Fairmont Hotels

5. Alisher Burkhanovich Usmanov

The richest man in Russia also happens to be an investor. Alisher Burkhanovch Usmanov has a big interest in the metal works and energy industry. Through his investment vehicle, he has purchased shares in wide-ranging sectors.

6. Ronald Perelman

Ronald is famously known as a corporate raider of the 80s, but he made his fortune through purchasing majority shares of big companies. He's the owner of AM General, the manufacturer of military crafts like the Humvee. His other investments touch upon many sectors like banks, entertainment, security, gaming, apparels, cosmetics, and publishing.

7. Mikhail Prokhorov

He's big on sports, particularly basketball, but Mikhail made his fortune by investing in the metals and mining sectors. He owns the investment company ONEXIM Group, with assets valued at $17 billion.

8. David Tepper

David Tepper was an investment banker working for Goldman Sachs before he quit and started his own fund, Appaloosa Management. He attracted many clients and made great investment decisions which saw high returns. His success secret was "Investing in the diciest of companies."

9. Philip Anschutz

Philip is definitely big on sports. He owns both Los Angeles Lakers and Los Angeles Kings and also played a huge part in starting Major League Soccer. He started in the oil business, but branched out into the railway industry, and now his investment claws have reached a wide range of sectors.

10. Stephen Schwarzman

Stephen Schwarzman started out as a banker at Lehman Brothers and was promoted to the position of managing director in a short length of time. In 1985, Stephen and his friends started the Blackstone Group, a company dedicated to acquisitions. Then the company got into leveraged buyouts of companies drawn from a wide range of industries.

Chapter 25:
Types of Securities

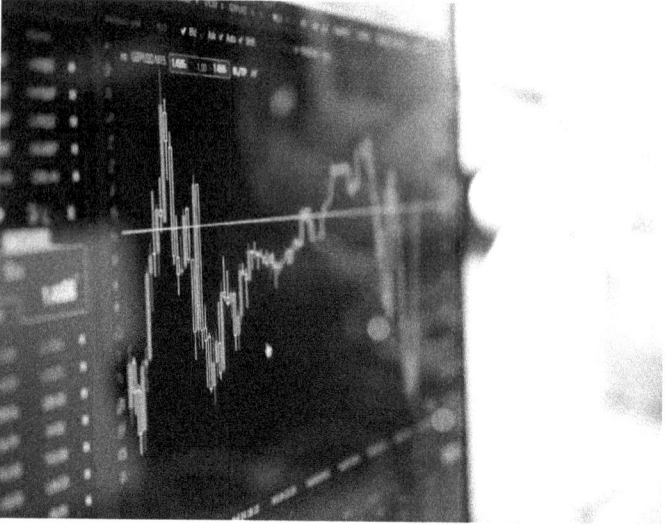

Securities are financial instruments that have value. They may be represented in part or the majority ownership of public companies, credit against governments, or any other ownership rights.

Shares. A shares represents an equity security. The holder of shares has ownership of part or majority of the company that issued the shares. Thus the holder of shares has the right of making contributions, whether intelligent or otherwise that affect the management of the company. In other words, a shareholder has a say. Investors buy shares with the intention of earning returns known as dividends. When a company earns a profit, part of the profit is distributed to shareholders as dividends. The amount of dividends paid out is decided by the shareholders and the board.

Bonds. A bond represents a debt security. When you purchase a bond, you may have no say in the company, but are entitled to receive an interest for a fixed period of time, and when your bond matures, you may receive your principal back. Also, the company may get you to agree to regular annual payments of the principal. The issuer usually pays interest once or twice per year.

Open-end funds. An open-end fund represents a diversified portfolio of securities investments. The securities investments are carefully selected and managed by a fund management company.

The fund does not have fixed capital and thus investors are the primary source of funds. Open-end funds may invest in local or international markets in all manner of securities. The fund manager determines the overall investment strategy. Open-end funds, are not normally traded on exchanges, and indeed there are very few exchanges where shares of open-end funds may be bought across the world. Open-end funds are normally purchased through fund management companies. But you may buy shares of open-end funds through a brokerage firm, and the investor may not pay any other fees but the broker's fees.

Index open-end funds. A fund manager allocates investors' resources into securities investments, thus making up an index. The yield of the index must be tracked.

Before units of index open-end funds are purchased, a declaration of accession must be signed. Afterward, assets are moved into a special account open at a bank. The fund management company will charge appropriate fees upon buy or sell executions. Investors are charged a fee by management and also pay for custodial services. The shares of open-end funds are bought and sold at net asset value, as calculated by the fund management company. Minor investors may buy index open-end funds at the market rate and are not charged entry or exit fees.

Closed-end funds; A closed-end fund involves investing resources into securities of other issuers. The management company gets to decide which securities to include in its portfolio.

Investment certificates. These are debt securities issued by a bank that offers an investor a set amount of money. But there are conditions. The issuers of investment certificates are mainly banks, and before you invest in investment certificate you might want to first check the credit rating of a bank.

Warrants. These are options offered by a joint-stock company that gives investors the right to buy a certain amount of the company's shares at a set price.

Chapter 26:

Rule #1: Never Lose Money!

You have probably heard of this quote by Warren Buffett, *"Rule No. 1: Never lose money. Rule No. 2: Don't forget rule No. 1."*

One of the biggest challenges for an investor is keeping their head level in the midst of chaos. A stock market is a chaotic place, no doubt.

For instance, a new company may go public and people will buy shares and be hopeful that the company will become a huge market player, except the company turns out to be a huge flop with zero public interest and no prospects of ever doing great business. So when investors see that, their base reaction is disappointment, yes. They get disappointed because this is yet another company threatening to lose their money.

Most investors rush to sell their stocks and at least break even or make a small loss. But what is the intelligent investor supposed to do? They are supposed to do their homework and evaluate the chances of survival of this company in the long run. The biggest companies never started off with a hoot after all.

As an investor, it is very hard not to lose money if you have not mastered your emotions. Actually, if you look at investments through the prism of emotions, that makes you a speculator, not an investor, and you set yourself up for failure.

When you commit your resources to an investment, there are many hazards to be fought.

The biggest of all is risky. You risk losing part or whole of your money.

But Warren Buffett says that risk can be eliminated, or at least can be brought to the minimum. You eliminate risk by being competent at what you are doing. When you know what you are doing, it won't be a stab in the dark anymore, but rather a sure bet.

The best way to become competent at what you are doing is through extensive research. It's amazing how lazy investors could get. When they come across a "promising investment" they just do a quick Google search to determine the parties involved, stalk their Facebook to see what they look like or how hilarious they are, and then they speed dial their broker to make the purchase.

Due diligence and fundamental analysis might not be very pleasurable activities, but they make up investment safety 101. An intelligent investor is his own best protector: he's more anxious about not losing money than he is about seeing a return.

Amidst all these, what is the place of gut feeling?

We often hear successful people tell us that they trusted their guts when it was time to make this big decision. But should investors also trust their guts where the viability of an investment is concerned?

Yes, they should do it and then back it up with fundamental analysis. In that sense, the spirit of fundamental analysis is to solidify your interest, rather than look for holes. However, if you come across red flags, then it's time to be rational and ignore your gut feeling.

After all, if you step back from an investment, it doesn't mean you lost, it means you still have the resources to invest in another project.

Never lose money.

Chapter 27:

Avoid These Mistakes that Even Smart Investors Make

An intelligent investor learns from the mistakes of others because the investment world can be unforgiving. Most of the time, the mistakes that ruin you are big mistakes, but they start small. These are some of the mistakes to keep guard against:

Having no plan. An investor should have a sense of direction. Having a plan alleviates anxiety and puts you in a place of power. You know what you are looking for. Your plan should address the following:

- **Goals and objectives.** Instead of having vague goals like, "I want to get rich doing this," say instead, "I want to make $100000 this year from the stock market."

- **Risks.** As an investor, you are going to have to make peace with risk. It will always be there. Thank goodness, because risk does a good job of chewing up incompetent investors. So, be aware of the risks that your investments might run into and either minimize them or be prepared to lose.

- **Measure.** Have a system in place to measure the effectiveness of your investment strategies.

Failing to diversify. But you must take care to diversify in the best-performing assets, otherwise you risk compounding failure and ending up in a much worse state. You also need to diversify across different asset classes. Diversification is the surest method of protecting yourself against major risk.

Investing in a short scale of time. Long-term investing is the mark of a true investor. However, most people seem to want to commit their resources to an investment only for so long, maybe its anxiety or life pressures, but they liquidate their securities very soon and move on to something else, thus killing off the momentum of their profits.

Wasting time on TV. Most of the news on TV is negative and it's deliberately so. Thought you'd find great investment wisdom on TV? Nope!

You cannot get worthy investment advice for free. You will have to subscribe to an authority (which costs money) or buy books or other related media.

Manager worship. Some people seem to think that the success of their investments is hinged upon the fund manager. It's true. Managers will select the securities, investment that their fund will invest in. In that sense, they play a big part in realizing success. However, when an investor becomes obsessed about who's running the fund, they have lost it. The important thing is that they are competent.

Timing the market. There is no such thing as timing the market. You only get burned trying to do that. If you have the resources, you just go into it and implement your strategy, focusing on portfolio diversification.

Neglecting your investments. Investments may be passive activity but it doesn't mean that it's one-strike affair. You need to check your investments regularly and rebalance your assets in order to stay aligned with your goals.

Not researching. If you haven't got the facts, you are susceptible to failure. Research makes up a big part of knowing what you are getting yourself into and thus arming yourself against risk.

When failure to research becomes a habit, it might cost you your investment career along with your resources, become another loser, and fellow investors will be looking at you and shaking their heads.

Chapter 28:
Glossary of Stock Market Terms

Agent: a securities firm that acts on behalf of its clients as a seller or buyer of a security.

Annual report: a publication that includes financial statements and operations report.

Arbitrage: the simultaneous buying of a security on one stock market and selling on another stock market in order to make a profit.

Assets: the valuable resources of a company or person such as securities, money, real estate, and equipment.

Bear market: When stock prices of a market fall down.

Bid: the highest price that a buyer is willing to pay for a stock.

Bonds: these are the promissory notes given by a public corporation or government to the lenders usually with a fixed amount within a fixed length of time.

Broker or brokerage firm: this is a securities firm or a registered financial advisor affiliated with a firm.

Bull market: where the stock prices are rising.

Capital: fixed assets, securities and other financial assets of an investor.

Capital gain or loss: the profit or loss after selling assets that are classified under income tax as capital assets.

Certificate: the physical document that indicates ownership of a stock, bond, and other security.

Closed-end investment fund: an investment trust that offers a set number of securities that trade on a stock exchange or in the over-the-counter market.

Commission: the fees that a broker requires for buying or selling securities on behalf of the investor.

Commodities: commerce products traded on an authorized commodities exchange.

Common shares: securities that represent a fraction of ownership in a company and generally bestow voting rights.

Daily price limit: the utmost price advance or dip for a futures contract in a trading session compared to the settlement price of the day before.

Day order: this is an order that is applicable only for the day it was entered.

Diversification: an investment style of minimizing risk whereby an investor purchases different types of securities.

Equities: stocks that represent a share in company ownership.

Underwriting: the purchase of securities for resale.

Venture capital: money raised by firms to finance business projects.

Warrant: a security that gives the holder the right to buy securities at a set price.

Yield: shown as a percentage, this is the measure of the return on an investment.

Conclusion

As Warren Buffett aptly put it, *"Rule No. 1: Don't lose money."*

The best way an investor may guard himself against losing money is by ensuring that they invest in securities where they are sure to win. Is that even possible? Yes. When you are competent at what you're doing, the element of risk is greatly minimized—eliminated, even. So the challenge is to become competent at what you're doing.

Every investor is helpless against "unsystematic risk." This is the risk that humans have no control over. It may visit upon investors in the form of inflation, market failure, political instability or an unfavorable legislation.

The best way to cover yourself against the cruel hands of risk is by spreading your portfolio. When you allocate your resources in different asset classes, you spread the risk, and thus you are less likely to be held back by the loss.

Fundamental analysis is important. Listening to your gut is not a bad thing. However, you should also evaluate a company's financial health before committing your resources to the company.

The main benefit of fundamental analysis is that it gives you a chance to find out whether a company is undervalued. An undervalued stock hasn't reached its intrinsic value. And so, buying an undervalued stock is a great investment decision, in the sense that when the prices go up you stand to gain a huge profit.

The worst trait in an investor is emotional instability. This kind of investor responds to negative market trends with fear-based actions.

The biggest quality in an investor is rationality.

Description

The stock market has its peculiarities. It's a world where a small matter has the potential of creating a massive impact. One thing added or one thing left out could be the difference between making a million dollars and losing it all.

There is no shortage of investors. The world has many of them. And you can be sure that some are extremely successful while others cry bitterly over their losses.

The reason why most investors fail is that they approach investing as though it were some lottery game. They are chance-takers. They have no plan. They stagger from one failed investment to another, taking stabs in the dark, and soon enough they lose all their money.

This book has been written to help you become an intelligent investor. An intelligent investor is not a chance-taker. An intelligent investor is a value investor who exploits market inconsistencies long before others have taken notice.

You will learn all the basics of the stock market investment and how to optimize your investments and realize the largest possible profits.

An investor should not turn himself into a speculator, for a speculator acts on his instincts rather than his intellect when executing trades.

The stock market is neither a mythical place beyond human understanding, nor a place reserved for people with special genetics. The investors who have made a fortune out of stock market are average people like everyone else except they took their time to understand everything before trying to get in the game.

There are many investments in the securities markets beyond stocks. You could invest in bonds and funds like mutual funds and index funds.

Investing in IPOs gives you a chance to own a slice of a company and in return, you play your part in providing the company with much-needed resources.

The best single thing an investor can do before taking up an investment deal is to conduct a fundamental analysis.

Fundamental analysis is the evaluation of a company's financial health with the intention of either solidifying your interest in the venture or finding out any red flag.

The strategies for succeeding as an investor are timeless. They worked a lifetime ago in the days of Ben Graham (the father of value investing) and they still work today.

www.ingramcontent.com/pod-product-compliance
Lightning Source LLC
Chambersburg PA
CBHW071418210326
41597CB00020B/3557